Christian Evidence Series of booklets

EVIDENCE FOR THE LOVE OF GOD

by

Richard Harries

*Bishop of Oxford
and former Dean of King's Colle*

Published by Mowbray for
THE CHRISTIAN EVIDENCE SOCIETY

Copyright © Richard Harries, 1987
ISBN 0 264 67115 5

First published 1987 for the Christian Evidence
Society by A.R. Mowbray & Co. Ltd., Saint Thomas
House, Becket Street, Oxford, OX1 1SJ.

Typeset by Getset (BTS) Ltd., Eynsham, Oxford
Printed in Great Britain by Tisbury Printing Works Ltd.,
Salisbury

Evidence for the Love of God

'DON'T KILL me mum.' These were the last words of an eight year old boy as his mother pushed him under the water in the bath and drowned him. Some years before this she had killed her two young babies but it was thought, mistakenly, that she was now in her right mind and her older boy was safe. Such incidents which, alas, we can read about every day, rock any religious faith we might have to the foundation. How on earth can there be a God of love behind a universe in which such appalling things happen?

The case against the idea that there is a power of love behind the universe is very strong. Indeed someone has suggested that the situation is like a detective story. All the evidence appears to point to a particular culprit but the good detective, by using his intelligence, is able to see that the situation is very different. So it is in life. On the surface all the evidence seems to point against the possibility that love created the universe. Droughts, famines, car crashes, murders, cancer, mental illness, senility – all these add up to a formidable case to answer. Yet, by careful thought this case can be answered and in the course of answering it surprisingly strong evidence *for* the idea of a God of love emerges.

The Price of Freewill

First, an obvious point. Much suffering in the world is caused by the negligence, weakness and deliberate wrong doing of human beings. If it is the will of God to create free beings, as opposed to robots or puppets, this is the price he and we have to pay. It is true that some philosophers have suggested that God could have created us free in such a way as we always freely chose to do right. On this view God would be like a hypnotist who told us all under hypnosis how we should act. We would think we were deciding things for ourselves but in fact we would have been programmed by God. It would have been quite possible to create a universe in which this happened. But there is one fatal flaw. God himself would know he had cheated. He, at least, would know that we were not acting with genuine freedom but only in response to suggestions given us under hypnosis.

If we value being able to make up our own mind and make our own decisions in life then we too have to pay the price of living in a world in which this is possible. We cannot have it both ways. We cannot both be free and have a world in which wrong choices do no damage. This point, if accepted, has wide implications. For much more suffering in the world is attributable to human beings than we sometimes allow. Take the millions of starving. The fact is that there *is* quite enough food in the world for everyone. But through millions of wrong choices which have brought about the rigid political and economic structures in which we live, there are mountains of surplus food in Europe and America, whilst those in Africa starve to death. Similarly, take the question of earthquakes. The rich can afford to live in earthquake free areas or in reinforced houses. It is the poor who cannot move or protect themselves. It is the poor who suffer.

Disease and Earthquakes

So a great deal of suffering in the world is caused by human beings. But not all of it. There is disease. There are natural disasters. Two points can be made about this. First, God does not simply make the world. He does something much more sophisicated. He makes the world make itself. He gives everything in the universe, from the sub-atomic particles of which matter is composed, through electrons, atoms, cells up to multi-cellular structures like ourselves, a life of its own. In fact, when we think about it, a life of our own is the only kind of life we could have. If we did not have a life of our own we would not exist at all and this is true of the atom and the amoeba as much as of us. God has given the basic elements of matter a life of their own and has weaved the universe from the bottom upwards through the free interplay of millions of forces. In all this interplay what we call accidents occur the whole time. But accidents are not in themselves harmful. Take the question of volcanoes and earthquakes. These occur because the star called earth, on which we live, has reached a particular stage in its cooling. This is also the stage which made it possible for life to emerge. If the earth was still molten there would be no life. If it had cooled to become a solid cold ball there would be no life. It has in fact cooled enough to allow a crust to form, on which life has been able to develop. But because it is a crust and not a solid ball the inner plates of the earth are still free to slide about a little, and the molten material inside the earth can on occasion find a way out of the crust. There is nothing wrong with these movements and eruptions in themselves. They are just examples of the millions and millions of clashes and combinations that occur every second at every level of the universe. They are not essentially different from the billowing of clouds or the movements of water in a stream.

God and the Laws of Nature
The second point is that in order to exist as the kind of creatures we are, capable of thinking and choosing, we need a relatively stable environment. I plan my day and make decisions in it on the basis of certain well-founded assumptions, that the sun will come up, that the laws of gravity will operate, that water will boil at a certain temperature and freeze at another one. The consequences of what I do, putting on the electric kettle or putting water in the freezer, are predictable. This means that there is a very strict limit on what God can do in the way of disrupting these scientific laws without frustrating his whole purpose in making the universe in the first place. It might be amusing to live in an Alice in Wonderland type of world but our amusement would only last a few seconds. If we suddenly started to shrink in an uncontrollable way or float up to the ceiling we literally

would not know whether we were coming or going. If we were born into that kind of environment we would never learn to think at all. For thinking necessitates continuity between one day's experience and the next. If a child went to school and was told that the sign A symbolised an aa sound and the next day was told that the same sign A symbolised an mm sound and the following day was told that the same sign really indicated an zz sound, that child would never learn to read, for learning involves building on present experience in a predictable way. So it is with our environment as a whole. Sometimes we long for God to 'intervene' to stop some terrible accident in a miraculous way, but where would it stop? Suppose you are driving along and a young child runs out in front of the car. Normally you would hit the child but a miracle occurs and you pull up short in 10ft instead of the expected 30ft. That would be wonderful. But what about the car just behind you? In order to prevent that car bumping into you, another miracle would have to occur. And what about the car behind that one? In other words a single alteration of the laws of nature (which are only laws in the sense that they are observed regularities on the basis of which we can make predictions) would have ramifications throughout the universe. And would it be fair to limit the miracle to one tiny point? If a miracle was performed to enable the first car to pull up in a few feet but not the second one, the driver of the second one could very well claim that it was unjust, for he had been driving along at the correct speed allowing for a proper stopping distance at that speed. He had not taken into account that a miracle would occur just in front of him and why should he?

The Self-Limiting of God

This is not in any way to deny that God works in his universe. According to Christian belief he is at the very heart of things, closer to us than our own breathing. Furthermore, he works out his purpose through us, particularly when we co-operate with him in prayer. Indeed prayer itself may allow

God to work through us in his universe in mysterious ways that we are not fully aware of. Nor is it to deny that full-blooded miracles, in the sense of a suspension of the laws of nature, may sometimes occur. The point is that there is a very severe limit to what God can do in this way without spoiling what it is all about – namely bringing into existence creatures like you and me, who are capable of thinking for ourselves and making real choices. For in order to exist as the kind of people we are, we need an environment characterised by continuity, stability, regularity and predictability.

The question arises, however, why did God make us as part of a material world? Much suffering arises from the fact that we are vulnerable creatures of flesh and blood, set in an environment whose regularity often seems very hard, as when a river floods and drowns many people. Why did not God simply create us as free spiritual beings like angels? No one really knows the answer to that question except God. All we can do is guess. The best guess comes from Austin Farrer. He argued that God bound us up with a physical universe in order to preserve our freedom in relation to himself. If we had been created like angels and set in the immediate presence of God we would have no freedom to respond to him or not. We would be drawn by his incandescent beauty and holiness like moths to a candle or metal filings to a magnet. So, in order that we might have real freedom of manouevre, God put us at a distance from himself. Not a physical distance, because that is impossible. God is closer to us than we are to ourselves. But a distance of knowing. He made us physical beings in a physical world to act as a kind of veil between us and himself. The result is that on this earth we have no immediate and overwhelming knowledge of God. Furthermore, we are born with a strong drive to preserve our life in being. We only come to a knowledge of God at all in so far as we are capable of growing out of our self-centredness and are willing to live before one who, by definition, makes a total difference to our lives. The knowledge of God is rarely overwhelming and inescapable. For most people there is only a flickering, dawning awareness which is always related to our willingness to know and love God. In this way God preserves our freedom and ensures that the pilgrimage we make is our own journey. (This guess has two implications, both of which I accept. First, angels are not as free as human beings. They are totally transparent to the bidding of God. Secondly, there was no fall of angels, for they were created perfect in the immediate presence of God.) We, however, have not been created perfect. We have instead been created with the possibility of achieving perfection of a different (and higher) kind than the angels. And we have not been created in the immediate presence of God. We have been made in such a way that we have to make our journey towards him.

So God has created a physical universe, which makes itself from the bottom upwards in ever more complex forms of life, until *we* emerge, as part of that physical universe, yet with the possibility of developing as rational, moral and spiritual beings; half ape, half angel, as Disrael put it. This physical universe is characterised by reliability and predictability. We are now, for example, beginning to be able to predict hurricanes, earthquakes, and volcanoes, and to take steps to avert their worst effects on us.

The Actions of God

But what, we might say, is God doing in all this? First, God is holding the whole universe in being and enabling each tiny constituent part of it to go on being itself. We tend to take this for granted. But why should each electron, atom and cell of the universe both be there and go on retaining its essential characteristics in such a way that it can combine to form higher forms of life? Religious believers claim this is so only because God, the source and fount of all being, holds everything in existence and does so in a way that reflects his own constancy. For the laws of nature, which we think of as so hard and impersonal, almost as an iron necessity, in fact reflect God's undeviating constancy and faithfulness. When the steam arises from a boiling kettle, or rain drops fall from the sky or a breeze dries the washing, these are expressions of the faithfulness of God, his steady constancy, his utter reliability.

Secondly, God himself feels the anguish of the universe. It is of the very nature of love to enter imaginatively into the situation of others and, to some extent, feel what they feel. God who is perfect love knows every point of the universe from the inside and bears it within his heart. The word sympathy comes from two Greek words meaning 'to suffer with'. God suffers with his creation. When Jesus was tortured to death this was an expression, in human terms, of the pain God bears eternally.

Thirdly, God is ceaselessly at work bringing good out of evil. When a tragedy occurs he inspires first sympathy and then practical action. He never stops in his work of making accident and disaster yield some good.

Fourthly, the purpose of God cannot finally be defeated. Christ died a terrible death on the cross apparently feeling that God has abandoned him. 'My God, My God why hast thou forsaken me?' But God raised him from the dead to live for ever in a new kind of way altogether, as an ever present spiritual presence. The purpose of love cannot finally be defeated.

Fifthly, God has promised us an eternal existence with himself. He knows each one of us through and through and he will recreate our real self in a form appropriate to an eternal existence. Heaven lies ahead for those who will appreciate it.

A God of Love
The case against the idea that there is a God of love behind the universe is very strong. Indeed so strong that it is only on the basis of these five points, taken together, that it is possible to hold such a belief. Belief in eternity can hardly be an optional extra, for example, when so many people die young with their potential unrealised. If there is no further state beyond this life for them to develop in how can we believe

there is a God of love? Similarly, if Christ was not raised from the dead how can we believe either in him or the God in whom he trusted? For he trusted his heavenly father to the bitter end, even through the darkness of despair. It is only on the basis of these five points that we can believe that love made the world. But these five points are also the evidence *for* the love of God. They provide not only the case for the defence but evidence for positive belief. The evidence that there is a God of love is based on our belief that the world has a genuine independence. We are not a dream of God or simply an expression of his body. His love is so great that he has made a world with a life of its own and brought to the light of consciousness creatures who even have the power to frustrate his purpose. But this is not an indifferent, impassive God. God bears our travail and anguish within himself. So much so that he has come amongst us and experienced as a human person the worst that life can do. Yet this is not a God who was irresponsible enough to make a world over which he would lose all control. Making the world was a huge risk but it was a risk he took in the confidence he could bring it to its natural fulfilment. Of this the resurrection of Christ is the expression and pledge. God's love cannot be defeated. He raised Christ from the dead and he will recreate each one of us anew for an eternal existence. As a father gives his children good gifts, so God will share with us his own immortality made manifest in Christ. This is very powerful evidence *for* the love of God. Believing in a God of love does not mean that horrible things do not happen. They do happen, all the time, for the reasons outlined earlier. The evidence for a God of love comes from a different source, from the five points just stated.

Is it worth it?
Although it is possible to understand some of the reasons why, if God was going to make creatures like us, the world has to have more or less the character of the world we know, it is still possible to wonder whether it is all worth it. 'Don't

8

kill me mum.' Was God really justified in creating a world in which he knew such things would happen. For even if there is an eternity ahead of that murdered child, nothing can change the fact that he was killed by his own mother and that he knew what was happening to him. This is the question of Ivan, one of the brothers in Dostoevsky's novel, *The Brother's Karamazov*. After recounting various stories of cruelty to children he asked if God was justified in making such a world. He then went on to argue that whatever harmony might be achieved in some heavenly future, nothing could justify such cruelty to children on the way. It wasn't that he disbelieved in God, he said. He just wanted to return his ticket. This is a powerful point, yet at least three things can be said which put a somewhat different perspective on the matter. First, the question of whether life is worth it or not is a question each one of has to answer for ourselves. No one can reply for us and we cannot presume to answer for them, however ghastly their circumstances seem to us. For when we come across someone in hospital, perhaps paralysed from the neck downwards, our instinctive reaction is that we could not bear to live life under such conditions. We would rather be dead. Yet often such people show extraordinary courage and even cheerfulness, enhancing life for others in a most moving way. Whether, despite everything, life is worth living is a question only they can answer. Secondly, the courage and endurance which so many show in life seems to witness to the fact that something desperately important is at stake in human life, that it is not simply a matter of weighing up the pleasure against the pain. If it was simply a matter of weighing up the pleasure against the pain far more people would commit suicide. But the vast majority of people do not commit suicide. They go struggling on with humour and fortitude, their lives, as someone once said, like flowers growing in a bed of concrete. In D. H. Lawrence's novel *Sons and Lovers* Paul Morel visits his mother, who is dying of cancer, and she chides him because his life is all struggle. She says she wants him to be happy. But Paul says that there is something more important than happiness and unhappiness; he wants to live. By that he did not mean live it up. He wanted to live with all the courage and creativity within him.

Thirdly, there are sometimes experiences in human life when a glorious goal makes the difficult journey to it seem worthwhile, as when a runner after years of hard training wins a gold medal at the Olympic games. Or there are times when a glorious experience can make the pain of the past drop away. As when an engaged couple who have been separated for a year and only able to communicate by 'phone and letter come together again. All the pain of missing one another and the inevitable misunderstandings suddenly fade into the background.

If at the end of the whole creative process, beyond space and time, when, as St Paul put it, God is all in all, everyone who has ever lived is able to bless God for their existence, then the unbiased critic must admit that God was justified in taking the risk of creating a universe. For all who have gone through the experience will say for themselves 'Praise the Lord O my soul, all that is within me, praise his holy name'. This would be heaven. Of course suffering will not be totally forgotten. In the stories of Christ's appearance to his disciples, the wounds remain. But they are healed and transfigured, taken into a new, deeper reality in which they too have a part to play. This vision of an ultimate state of affairs in which all is well is a hope. But it is a hope that is witnessed to not only by the Christian faith but by the practical example of countless millions of people, of all faiths and none, who live lives with great courage. For they seem to have an intuitive sense that something vastly important is at stake in all this human travail. In old fashioned language what is at stake is the making of our eternal souls.

A Practical Answer
On Karl Marx's grave in Highgate cemetery are carved his famous words 'Philosophers have only interpreted the world, the point is, however, to change it'. Christians have

much sympathy with that statement. For they do not offer a philosophical answer to the problem of suffering, as though it were something to be resigned to. They offer a vision of an ultimate state of affairs in which suffering as we know it no longer exists, a state of affairs which has to be worked for. It is true that the new heaven and earth of which the Bible speaks go beyond our space and time but they have to be reached for and built up on this earth. The answer to the problem of suffering is not an idea or a theology but an actual state of affairs, which does not yet exist, but which offers us a vision of what, under God, can come about if we co-operate with God in his work. There are some very important practical implications of this.

First, suffering is contrary to the will of God. In the Gospels Jesus is shown healing the physically and mentally sick, casting out demons, calling sinners to change their ways. His ministry is an invasion of the forces of goodness and light against all that blights and hurts human life. There may be a sense in which God is responsible for everything, in that he created the universe. But a sharp distinction has to be made between what God directly wills and what he merely permits as part of his overall purpose. So a parent may be responsible for giving his child permission to drive the family car. But he in no sense wills the subsequent accident that unfortunately occurs. God wills the universe to exist, he lets it be with a life of its own. But he does not will suffering; on the contrary, he opposes it. Christ, the image of God, brings life and health. So Christians, following his example, have founded hospitals, leper colonies, hospices and all manner of institutions dedicated to relieving the sick.

Secondly, God is ceaselessly at work bringing good out of evil and we are called to co-operate with him in this task. For it is the particular work of God not only to oppose all that mars human life but to make what mars our lives yield some good fruit. So sickness can bring about sympathy and practical support from friends and a deeper understanding of life from the sufferer. Here we have to be very careful. Whilst it is true that many good qualities and actions can come out of sickness or tragedy, God does not design horrible situations in order to bring this good out of them. Such a god would be intolerable. If a friend tripped us up on the stairs and broke our leg in order to see whether we would develop qualities of patience and endurance under adversity we would not think much of his or her friendship: indeed we would not call him or her a friend. So with God. God, like a good friend, wants things to go well with us. He is not about to pull the carpet from under us to see how we will react. For good breeds more good than evil can. A comfortable home, with enough to eat, caring parents and an interest in sport or culture is much more likely to give children a chance to develop as healthy personalities than a home that is impoverished or stricken in one way or another. The parents in such a home may be very caring but if they are continually worried about money, have little time to give to their children because they have to work so hard, if they live in poor physical surroundings or are stricken with mental illness, then the children are likely to be affected. Good breeds more good than evil can. It is the particular mercy of God to make even evil yield some good.

Everyone knows someone who under adversity has developed admirable qualities. We have all been involved in tragic or difficult situations which have brought the best out of people. This is all summed up in some lines of the poet Edwin Muir. He contrasts our sad world with the apparently perfect conditions of the garden of Eden, but concludes:

> But famished field and blackened tree
> Bear flowers in Eden never known;
> Blossoms of grief and charity
> Bloom in these darkened fields alone.
> What had Eden ever to say
> Of hope and faith and pity and love. . . .
> Strange blessings never in Paradise
> Fall from these beclouded skies.

There is a tightrope to walk here. God does not will suffering. On the contrary he wills us to relieve and eliminate it, so far as we can. Yet out of suffering can come hope and faith and pity and love. God did not design the beclouded skies in order that the strange blessings might fall from them. Yet fall they do, making life look very different. The weighing of goods and evils is notoriously difficult and should not be done. A husband who has just lost a dearly loved wife does not want to be told that he has become a much deeper, more understanding person as a result. He would rather have his wife back. A man whose son has been killed in a motor bike accident may spend the rest of his life helping youth clubs and do much good work. But he would rather have his son back. Yet, if there is an eternal destiny, the good which people see coming out of evil will one day find its proper place. For if we have been made to grow more and more like God, so that we can live with him in the communion of saints, the deepening of a person in a bereavement or the good work that people undertake as a result of a tragedy are considerations of ultimate significance.

Living in Faith

The thoughts put forward here are only of very limited use and no use at all when a person is in anguish. When a person is afflicted with physical or mental pain they want understanding and practical help. They do not want religious consolation or attempts to 'justify the ways of God to men'. Nevertheless, there is a limited use for the kind of considerations adduced here on other occasions. For, as has been admitted, the case against the idea that love made the world is a formidable one. Unless something sensible is said, faith can ebb away and hope die. There is no intellectual solution to the problem of suffering and certainly no knock down arguments. All that is possible is to say enough to go on living in faith and hope and love. For, paradoxically, the very strength of the case against the notion of a god of love reveals more clearly the evidence *for* a God of love. This evidence, as considered earlier, has five features. First, God has given us a real independence. He has *created* us rather than dreamt us. Secondly, God himself feels our anguish with us. Thirdly, he is ceaselessly at work forcing even evil to yield some good. Fourthly, as the resurrection of Christ reveals, his purpose cannot finally be defeated. And fifthly, God has promised us an eternal existence, if we are ready to receive it. A character in a novel by Rebecca West says at one point 'What's the good of music if there's all this cancer in the world?' To this someone else responds 'What's the harm of cancer, if there's all this music in the world?' Music can lift people into a dimension in which life seems very different. This is even more true of the love of God. A knowledge of the love of God does not stop tragedy being tragedy or suffering suffering. There is no glossing over, no pretending that all is for the best. For manifestly all is not for the best; a great deal is for the worst. But the love of God, of which we all have some practical proof in the sheer existence of our own being, but which is definitively disclosed in the life, death and resurrection of Christ together with the promises to us inherent in Christ, is a kind of music which makes us see, in our best moments, what really matters and what does not matter quite so much.

There is no intellectual solution. Instead the Christian faith offers a vision of what the love of God is in the course of achieving. We are called to co-operate with that love by relieving suffering, eliminating its causes in poverty and disease and by responding to things going wrong in as constructive and positive way as possible. For so it is that God's purpose is furthered. A sense of how much suffering there is in life can lead us to deny our maker or to care for his world. The more we care, the more conscious we will be of the affliction which besets us. But the more we care the more certain we will be that the world which is afflicted is good. And in caring we will be at one with the caring of God.